AF095657

THE POETRY OF
IRIDIUM

The Poetry of Iridium

Walter the Educator

Silent King Books

SILENT KING BOOKS

SKB

Copyright © 2024 by Walter the Educator

All rights reserved. No part of this book may be reproduced in any manner whatsoever without written permission except in the case of brief quotations embodied in critical articles and reviews.

First Printing, 2024

Disclaimer
This book is a literary work; poems are not about specific persons, locations, situations, and/or circumstances unless mentioned in a historical context. This book is for entertainment and informational purposes only. The author and publisher offer this information without warranties expressed or implied. No matter the grounds, neither the author nor the publisher will be accountable for any losses, injuries, or other damages caused by the reader's use of this book. The use of this book acknowledges an understanding and acceptance of this disclaimer.

"Earning a degree in chemistry changed my life!"
- Walter the Educator

dedicated to all the chemistry lovers, like myself, across the world

In the deep expanse where stars ignite,

IRIDIUM

There gleams a metal, rare and bright.

IRIDIUM

Iridium, born of cosmic fire,

IRIDIUM

In the heart of stars, it does aspire.

IRIDIUM

From supernovae's explosive dance,

IRIDIUM

It emerged with an elegant stance.

IRIDIUM

A precious gift from the universe's hand,

IRIDIUM

Iridium, a jewel in the celestial band.

IRIDIUM

Within the Earth's crust, it does reside,

IRIDIUM

In hidden veins, it does abide.

IRIDIUM

A silent witness to ages past,

IRIDIUM

Iridium, a relic that will forever last.

IRIDIUM

Its lustrous sheen, a sight to behold,

IRIDIUM

A story of mysteries yet untold.

IRIDIUM

In laboratories, it finds its place,

IRIDIUM

Aiding in discoveries, expanding our grace.

IRIDIUM

With atoms arranged in orderly arrays,

IRIDIUM

Iridium commands with majestic displays.

IRIDIUM

A conductor of heat and electricity's flow,

IRIDIUM

It illuminates pathways where knowledge does grow.

IRIDIUM

In catalytic converters, it plays its part,

IRIDIUM

Purifying emissions, a guardian of the heart.

IRIDIUM

Catalyzing reactions with effortless grace,

IRIDIUM

Iridium, a champion in the chemical race.

IRIDIUM

In medicine's realm, it lends a hand,

IRIDIUM

Guiding treatments, a beacon on demand.

IRIDIUM

Implanted in devices, it serves with care,

IRIDIUM

Extending lives with expertise rare.

IRIDIUM

In the artist's palette, it adds allure,

IRIDIUM

Infusing pigments with a gleaming allure.

IRIDIUM

A touch of iridescence, a stroke of delight,

IRIDIUM

Iridium, the painter's silent knight.

IRIDIUM

In the annals of history, it leaves its mark,

IRIDIUM

A testament to resilience, a spark in the dark.

IRIDIUM

From ancient times to modern days,

IRIDIUM

Iridium's legacy forever stays.

IRIDIUM

So let us marvel at this element divine,

IRIDIUM

A symbol of resilience, a gem to shine.

IRIDIUM

In the tapestry of the cosmos, it weaves its thread,

IRIDIUM

Iridium, a testament to life's journey ahead.

IRIDIUM

In laboratories and factories, it toils away,

IRIDIUM

A silent sentinel, come what may.

IRIDIUM

But in the hearts of dreamers, it sparks a flame,

IRIDIUM

Iridium, forever bound to its cosmic claim.

IRIDIUM

So let us raise our voices high,

IRIDIUM

In praise of iridium, reaching for the sky.

IRIDIUM

ABOUT THE CREATOR

Walter the Educator is one of the pseudonyms for Walter Anderson. Formally educated in Chemistry, Business, and Education, he is an educator, an author, a diverse entrepreneur, and he is the son of a disabled war veteran. "Walter the Educator" shares his time between educating and creating. He holds interests and owns several creative projects that entertain, enlighten, enhance, and educate, hoping to inspire and motivate you.

Follow, find new works, and stay up to date
with Walter the Educator™
at WaltertheEducator.com

www.ingramcontent.com/pod-product-compliance
Lightning Source LLC
LaVergne TN
LVHW052005060526
838201LV00059B/3847